Angel Encounters

True Stories of Angelic Interventions

Guardian Angels, Messengers, Rescues, and Guides to the Other Side

Conrad Bauer

ISBN: 978-1721665075

Printed in the United States

MAPLEWOOD
– PUBLISHING –

Contents

Angels Among Us

A motorist is trapped on the side of the road in the middle of a winter storm with no one to help them. Then, out of nowhere, a mysterious figure appears to guide them through the blizzard. A family falls on hard times until a kind stranger shows them how to overcome their meager circumstances. A woman has a near death experience in which a being of pure light guides her to heaven. We have all heard such stories. Could there be any truth in them? And if so, just who are these beings of grace and kindness that seem to randomly visit the select few?

Who are these angelic strangers that some of us have entertained unaware? Who are these angels among us? This book presents many accounts of those who claim to have been waited upon by these celestial visitors from beyond. If we are to believe them, we will have to admit that there is a lot to the natural world that our limited knowledge still doesn't quite understand. And so, if you are ready and willing to suspend your rational judgment and make that leap of faith, come along as we discover the angels among us.

Angels as our Friends and Guardians

At first glance, the phrase 'guardian angel' may seem like a quaint colloquialism. However, there are countless stories of people all throughout history who claim to have had their own personal angelic protector, friend, guardian and guide. Before we discuss anything else, let's dive into the stories of these special guardian angels. They come when they are most needed and least expected. If you are ever in trouble and need some help, just look to your guardian angel.

Keisha Williams Gets Help from the Colonel

When Keisha Williams, a young mother of three, found herself lost and alone in a foreign country, she certainly felt like she could use a guardian angel. And according to her account of what happened, that is precisely what she got! Her husband Robert was in the U.S. military during the 1980s, and at the time he was stationed at a Cold War era army base in West Germany. After being there for six months, he was able to request that his wife and children join him in Europe.

Keisha had never left the country before, and it was going to be a big transition for her to go overseas for the first time. But she was more than willing to sacrifice some of the comforts of home if it meant their family could be reunited. Soon enough, Keisha was on board a plane with her little children in tow, heading to West Germany. It was difficult for her from the very beginning. Although she had attended a crash course in German before leaving, several failed attempts at speaking with the German flight attendants convinced her that her capacity for Deutsche was woefully inadequate.

So other than yelling at her kids to stop pestering each other, she remained completely silent for the rest of the flight. She was immensely relieved when the plane finally landed, and after getting her baggage and her children in order, she made her way through the airport to meet her husband. The only trouble was that her husband was nowhere to be seen. She scanned the crowds of eager family members waiting to meet the new arrivals, but her husband's face wasn't among them. She felt the beginnings of panic, but she quickly pushed these feelings aside, telling herself that her husband would be there—he was probably just running late.

Trying her best to remain positive, she pushed her luggage and pulled her children toward a nearby bench to sit and wait. But as the minutes wore on, her worry grew. Soon she decided to call her husband's base to make sure that everything was alright. But upon walking over to the pay phone, she realized that she didn't have the slightest idea how to use it. All of the instructions were in German, and the phone required German coins.

With panic and despair threatening to seize her completely, she mentally cried out, "Oh God, please help me! What am I going to do?" Immediately after this desperate cry for help, a mysterious stranger seemed to appear out of nowhere to offer assistance. In an airport in which she had heard nothing but German, she was surprised when a man asked in perfect, fluent English, "Is there something I can help you with, ma'am?" The stranger was in his late 50s to early 60s, wearing a suit, tie, and glasses, with a short white beard and a well-manicured head of all-white hair.

The thought didn't occur to her at the time, but in retrospect she realized that the man actually had an uncanny resemblance to Colonel Sanders of Kentucky Fried Chicken! There seems to be a common thread in many stories of angelic visitation in which these beings seem to take on whatever shape is most comforting and non-confrontational for their host. Is this what was happening to Keisha? Did an angel drop down from heaven, read her mind, and decide she would be receptive to someone who looked like Colonel Sanders from KFC? But although this mysterious man wasn't advertising chicken, he was ready to render some serious aid.

After Keisha explained her plight, the man expertly worked the pay phone for her, dialed the number she had on hand, and dropped a few German coins into the slot. After a moment, he handed the phone to Keisha, and she was relieved to hear the base commander on the other end. The commander informed her that her husband had been in a car accident and was in the hospital being treated for a broken leg. It wasn't anything serious, but he would have to be on bed rest for a few days, and that was why he wasn't able to make it to the airport.

Keisha ended her call with a mixture of relief and frustration. She was relieved to know that her husband was alright, but she was frustrated to be stranded at the airport. Couldn't they have sent someone to pick her up? Unfortunately, Keisha Williams seemed to be on her own—that is, except for the angelic Colonel Sanders who was still standing by patiently. As if he intuitively knew the turmoil she was feeling, this man (or angel in disguise, if you will) patted Keisha on the back and told her, "Don't worry, ma'am. I will get a train for you so you can get to the base."

He then reached into his beat-up old briefcase and pulled out a bottle of water. It was a small gesture of kindness that meant a lot. Keisha hadn't drunk anything the whole flight and was incredibly thirsty. Did the angel sense this as well? She thanked him for the water and quickly drank it down. Many of us might be leery of drinking anything handed to us by a random stranger, but according to Keisha, this man had a way of soothing her nerves and calming her suspicions. She felt completely at ease with him, as if she had nothing at all to fear from being in his company.

This guardian angel then led her out of the airport terminal and hailed a taxi for her, speaking what seemed to be fluent German. He was obviously bilingual; even though Keisha didn't know what was being said, she could tell that he was effortlessly explaining her situation in great detail and instructing the taxi driver to take her to the train station.

After making sure everything was in order, and that Keisha, her children, and her belongings were safely inside the cab, the man shut the door for them like a perfect gentleman. Then he simply smiled, waved, and walked away. Keisha wished she'd had a chance to thank the stranger for his kindness, but she was relieved to think she would be able to make it to the base after all.

About 30 minutes later her cab arrived at the train station as planned. But as Keisha and her children piled out of the taxi and she began to look around at the large, complex train station, she felt discouraged once again. Her panic returned as she realized that she had no idea where to go! Everything she heard and saw around her was in German, and she had no idea how to navigate through the chaotic environment. Completely lost both in the literal and metaphorical sense, Keisha felt like she was about to burst into tears right then and there. But then something made her glance at the train station schedule she had been clutching in her hands. She hadn't noticed it before, but the helpful man at the airport had apparently written painstaking instructions for her in clear and perfectly legible English!

She wasn't sure when he'd had the time to do this—but her guardian angel had managed to come through for her once again! As she saw it, her mind shouted out in pure joy, "God bless him! God bless that guy for doing this for us!" Keisha followed the directions as she understood them and boarded a train to head out to the base. But just as she and her kids were getting settled into their seats, none other than their guardian angel from the airport poked his head into their car to tell them, "Sorry to bother you, but you are on the wrong train."

Before the astonished Keisha could say another word, this supposed angel then boarded the train, grabbed her luggage, and literally began leading her by the hand to the train that would take her to her husband's army base. She couldn't believe it. The whole situation was humanly impossible. The last time she had seen him, he was heading back into the airport—and now, many minutes and miles later, he was right there in front of her at the train station. How did he get there? Furthermore, how did he happen to know they were on the wrong train?

Before she could give voice to her astonishment, her mysterious angel pointed at the train's conductor in the car in front of them and informed her, "He speaks a little English. If you have any questions, he will help you from here." Her guardian angel then simply smiled and stepped off the train. Keisha went to the door of the car to yell after him and thank him once again for all of his help, but to her astonishment, he was gone. It was as if he had just vanished into thin air.

She searched the crowds of people waiting for their trains, but her guardian angel was nowhere to be seen. She made it to the base later that evening just as her helper had told her she would. When she was reunited with her husband and told him the story, he was still a little groggy from his pain medicine, and all he could think to say was, "God must have sent you an angel." To this day, Keisha sincerely believes this to be the case: That helpful stranger was indeed her guardian angel.

This would have been a perfect ending to this angelic account—but there is more. Right after her husband uttered those words, a soldier came into the room clutching a big bucket of Kentucky Fried Chicken and shouting, "Hey guys! Are you hungry? Just got us a bunch of fried chicken from the only KFC in West Germany!" It was actually Keisha's little 4-year-old daughter who spoke what she already knew. As the girl pointed at the face emblazoned across the bucket of fried chicken, she cried, "Mommy! That's him—that's the man who helped us!" Fighting back tears, all Keisha could do was nod, "I know baby—I know."

Lorna Byrne's Angelic Entourage

Self-proclaimed Irish mystic Lorna Byrne has perhaps logged more hours with her guardian angels than anyone else on record! Although she is dyslexic and claims to have extreme difficulty reading and writing, Lorna penned one of the best-selling books on angels of the 21st century with her 2008 hit *Angels in My Hair*. In this book she reveals that she has secretly been in contact with angels since she was six months old. She claims that she can recall the moment that the angels first introduced themselves to her as she lay in her crib, and that they've stuck with her ever since.

The angels allegedly give her an insider's view into the spiritual workings of her life and the lives of those around her. When she was a child, the knowledge she was given by her angelic instructors was often a bit too much too handle and would overwhelm her emotionally—as was the case when she was informed that her best friend's father was going to pass away. It was a particularly sad bit of angelic insider information for her guardians to impart to her. Lorna's best friend Alice had just found out that her father, who worked in faraway England, had just gotten a job close to home in Ireland and would be "home for good".

The angels, however, told Lorna that Alice's father would indeed be home for good, but not his earthly home—he was going home to heaven. Whether anyone would actually believe her or not, Lorna knew better than to divulge such devastating news, and so she kept the secret knowledge to herself. On the exact day of the man's passing, Lorna was playing outside when she saw a brilliant beam of light strike the top of Alice's house. As she looked closer she could see angels descending and ascending up this beam of light.

Similar to the biblical account of Jacob's Ladder, a portal seemed to have been opened with these beings traveling back and forth between this world and the next. As she stared at these strange happenings, she heard an angel tell her to look directly at the outside wall of the home. The walls then dissolved and the entire home became transparent. She could now see what was going on inside: Alice's mother was sobbing and shaking the lifeless body of Alice's father. Lorna then noticed the dead man's disembodied spirit in the corner of the room. It was being gently embraced by angels and two other spirits that appeared to be somehow related to the deceased.

In later years, her angel guardians often positioned themselves as teachers giving her a front row seat to observe the inner workings of life, death, and everything in between. For the most part she kept this secret knowledge to herself.

The catalyst for her to come out with her story was the death of her husband at the age of 47. The angels had long ago predicted his passing. In fact, according to Lorna, it was the angels that had even first introduced her to him. Lorna claims that when she was just 10 years old, the angels got her attention and conjured up a vision of a handsome young man before informing her that this was the man that she was going to marry.

She didn't actually meet her future husband until several years later, but the man she met was indeed the very same person the angels had shown her in the vision. Unfortunately, the angels also had some startling news to impart about Lorna's soul mate. They told her that he would only live to be 47, and Lorna claims to have lived with this knowledge the entire time she was married to her husband.

She never told him that she knew when he would expire, reasoning that it would only have made him dread the future and would have lessened the precious time he had on this earth. It would seem that having to figure out what to do with such profound insights is just part and parcel of hanging out with angels your whole life.

Among the angelic host that serves as her guides are none other than the Archangels Michael and Gabriel. Lorna has never questioned why she was chosen by these celestial beings; she just accepts their stewardship in her life for what it is.

Lorna has recently stunned the world once again with her angelic teachings, claiming that the angels gave her a prophecy concerning the ongoing conflict in Syria. She claims that the angels gave her a vision in which she saw countless people being killed in a worldwide apocalyptic conflagration triggered by the involvement of world powers in Syria. After much of humanity had been devastated by this future Armageddon, the survivors were left to scratch their heads, wondering why no one had done enough to defuse this situation.

She says that the overall feeling of these beleaguered inheritors of the destruction was that their leaders simply hadn't done enough. She warns us that the vision that her angelic guides showed her could become a reality if we aren't careful—but it doesn't have to. As the Syrian conflict heats up, and Russia and the United States position themselves and their proxies in increasingly aggressive stances in this protracted struggle, let's hope that this grim vision of the future given to Lorna by her angelic entourage does not come to pass after all.

Bill Burman's Special Friends

Ever since he was a kid, Bill Burman has intuitively felt that someone was watching over him. And after several close calls with death early on in life, he has the kind of testimony that would seem to back up those claims. The first instance in which he believes his guardian was looking out for him occurred when he was no more than three years old. He was living with his family in a small, modest house during a period in which his parents had hit some rather hard times.

In fact, they barely had enough money to pay the bills, and once they were paid there was absolutely nothing left over. As Bill tells it, the only reason his family didn't starve was thanks to government assistance programs that provided basic monthly staples such as cheese, butter, flour, and milk. When Bill talks about being raised on government cheese he's not joking—he's telling the truth! But despite the destitute surroundings in which he lived, as a child Bill always felt especially blessed. He seemed to have direct communion with the divine at a young age.

Some would call them angels, but as a small child Bill didn't know that kind of terminology. All he knew was that the beings of light that visited him were his playmates. The earliest recollection he has of seeing these angelic entities was when he was going to the bathroom. It sounds utterly ridiculous, but this is precisely how Bill remembers it.

The fine human art of using a toilet had just recently been taught to the precocious 3-year-old, but that's beside the point. As Bill describes it, as soon as he shut the bathroom door to "go potty" he saw "liquid light" descend through the bathroom ceiling. The liquid light hung in the air over various parts of the bathroom, where it transformed into what can only be termed as angels. It seems that the entities were just waiting for a moment in which Bill was alone in order to present themselves to him, and his bathroom break was as good an opportunity as any.

It would have been hard for an adult mind to comprehend the sight, but somehow in Bill's childish mind he didn't question the event. For him, the phenomenon seemed completely normal, and he simply accepted it at face value. Perhaps this is why children are sometimes said to see aspects of reality that adults simply can't fathom. Keeping their eyes wide open with childlike acceptance, they see what the adult dismisses outright as an impossibility.

At any rate, whenever these beings made their spontaneous appearances, Bill was never fearful or afraid. He maintains that he always felt nothing but love and kindness from them. He always had the distinct feeling that these beings were his friends who guarded, protected and watched over him. In essence, they were his guardian angels.

These protective angels would soon become quite handy in Bill's young life, because shortly after these initial visitations, tragedy struck. It had been a cold winter, and the family's heat had been shut off for nonpayment. In a desperate attempt to keep the drafty old house warm, Bill's parents had installed a kerosene heater. He dad had put the heater in the living room, off to the side near the hall. He hoped this would be a safe place for it to churn out its warmth over the course of the cold night. But unfortunately, it wasn't far enough out of the way for a rambunctious toddler like Bill, and soon he and that heater would have a near lethal collision.

On one fateful Saturday, Bill had gotten up early in the morning before his parents had woken up and wandered into the living room. With the sleep still in his eyes, he scanned the room looking for something to play with. Off against the side wall he spotted his favorite toy, a model dump truck he had left out the night before. Skipping and hopping to get his toy, Bill managed to ensnare his foot on the rug under the coffee table. He sprawled forward, lunging toward the kerosene heater—and from the trajectory of his fall, he should have fallen right on top of it and received severe burns on most of his body.

But according to Bill, as he fell toward the kerosene heater, time seemed to slow down. Everything was in slow motion as he neared the heater, and right before he was about to strike it head on, he saw that same liquid light drop out of the ceiling and deposit itself next to him. In an instant, a golden hand emerged from the light and gently pushed him ever so slightly to the left. It wasn't a powerful shove, just a gentle nudge, but it was enough to prevent a straight-on collision with the heater.

Instead, Bill just brushed against it, ever so slightly burning his arm. The jolt of pain was still enough to cause him to scream and cry out, and his startled parents rushed into the living room to tend to him. By the time they arrived, Bill's guardian angel was long gone, but Bill would never forget how his special friends had looked after him.

Angels in Times of Crisis

Whether we face war, famine, natural disaster, or a crisis of a more personal nature, angels have been reported to emerge in the midst of this dire chaos. Here we take a look at some of the most fascinating accounts of direct angelic intervention during trying times of crisis.

Flight 93's Field of Angels

If any single event could be defined as a "time of crisis", the terrorist attacks of September 11, 2001, certainly qualify. The details of that day are still etched in our collective memory, even years after the fact. Those of us who are old enough can usually remember exactly where we were and what we were doing on the day of that atrocity. And former FBI agent Lillie Leonardi's recollection of that September morn is crystal clear.

She had woken up to find her government-issue car with a dead battery and called the Bureau's mechanic to bring a new one. While waiting for him to arrive, she flipped on her television and saw the breaking news that a plane had just smashed into one of the twin towers of New York's World Trade Center. Like millions of others across the country, she then watched in horror as another plane collided with the second tower. To her complete disbelief, word soon came that a third plane had struck the Pentagon in Virginia, while a fourth hijacked plane was believed to be still at large.

Just what was happening? Multiple planes falling out of the sky? Was this the end the world? If Lillie had these thoughts as she watched the disturbing news feed of the events, she certainly wasn't the only one. Many of us felt as if the world was coming apart at the seams. But for Lillie, the events of 9/11 became personal when the newscaster finally rattled off the whereabouts of that fourth plane. The airplane which would forever be known as Flight 93 had just crashed into a field in the desolate wilds of Western Pennsylvania, near the sleepy little town of Shanksville.

This was not far from the Pittsburgh FBI office where Lillie worked. Now the terror of 9/11 had come to her home turf. As soon as her car was up and running, she headed straight to the FBI building, expecting to be assigned to the scene of the crash. Sure enough, she was soon ordered to escort a special mobile command unit to Shanksville. They raced to the scene, joining state police, firefighters, and other emergency personnel that had assembled around the wreckage of what had been an airplane full of humanity.

Of those unfortunate souls on board, Lillie could find no sign—all the first responders saw was a smoking crater in the ground. The jet fuel ignited fire had already been put out, and the cockpit and other wreckage were almost entirely buried in the charred earth.

But in the midst of this desolation, Lillie's attention was drawn to something else entirely. As she stared at the smoldering remains of the plane, she began to see strange flashes of light in the distance, out of the corner of her eye.

She turned her head to the left of the wreckage and saw a swirling "mist of light". She fixed her gaze on this misty haze, and the next thing she knew she was staring at what appeared to be an entire legion of angels! Right by the wreckage of Flight 93, she could see clear as day an entire army of angels gathered together as if they were about to march to battle! Leading this angelic host was what Lillie described as an archangel—an angelic general giving orders to the other angels under his command.

He had a giant sword in his right hand, pointed at the ground but at the ready. Drawing upon her Catholic faith, which emphasizes angelic hierarchy, Lillie immediately identified this archangel as Michael, the holy warrior and enforcer of divine order. She says that although the angels were stern-faced and somber as they received their instructions from Michael, they still left an impression of being completely benevolent, loving and kind.

As she gazed upon these celestial beings it was as if time stood still, and every single movement and gesture from this angelic host was forever burned into her memory. But no one else around her seemed to be able to see these fantastic phantasms. Worrying that the stress of the day was getting to her, she attempted to find a way to rationalize a vision that defied logical explanation.

She was interrupted when the wreckage of Flight 93 suddenly erupted into an inferno once again. Lillie and her associates were abruptly ordered off the field by the FAA, so she had no choice but to leave her angelic visitors behind. Just before she climbed into her vehicle to leave, she looked back toward the field where she had seen the angel army, but they were no longer present.

At this point, she really began to wonder if what she thought she had seen was nothing more than a mirage, or a stress-induced hallucination. Deep inside, she prayed to God for a sign to let her know whether it had been real. Standing by her car, she then happened to look down and see a bible lying on the ground near her feat. Just singed at the edges, this good book had apparently survived the crash relatively unscathed. As Lillie stared down at this bible, the wind suddenly blew it open to Psalm 23. As this seasoned FBI agent read the words "The Lord is My Shepherd," she knew in her heart that what she had seen was indeed real.

She wasn't so sure her colleagues would agree with her, however, and for many years she kept the sighting to herself. Even so, the vision bolstered her with the renewed sense of confidence and purpose that she needed. She knew that no matter what happened, that army of angels was keeping watch. The guardians she observed in that forlorn field in Western Pennsylvania on that dark day of September 11th were doing their very best to shepherd a traumatized humanity through one of the worst times of crisis it had ever known.

The Angels of Cokeville Elementary

If ever anyone was in need of an angel during a time of crisis, it was the teachers and students of Cokeville Elementary who were being held hostage on May 16, 1986. They were the victims of a mad married couple, David and Dorra Young. David was a disgruntled ex-cop, and his wife Dorra was a two-time divorcee who had become embittered by her unsuccessful marital history and the untimely loss of her son from one of her previous marriages.

Both David and Dorra were adamant atheists, with a mutual interest in topics such as reincarnation and philosophy. A big part of their personal philosophy was David's concept that reality was merely an invention of the human mind, and that we are only here because we perceive ourselves to be here. With such mystical beliefs, David and Dorra had lost their fear of death, since they believed life itself to be something that they just dreamed up in their heads.

David and Dorra's misbegotten metaphysical meanderings eventually became more and more erratic, and David began to call for them to take dramatic action to wake up the world to the reality he believed in. He called this perceived tipping point "the Biggie". For all of David Young's supposed intellect and his belief in his superiority to others, his plan was rather simple. He was going to visit violence and terror upon his Wyoming community in order to get people to pay attention to him.

For all of his high-minded philosophical talk, he was really no different than any other egocentric megalomaniac wishing to gain infamy by taking out his ill-will upon his fellow man. The target he chose was a small, nondescript elementary school in Cokeville, Wyoming. On the morning of May 16th, David and Dorra, both heavily armed, loaded a homemade bomb onto a shopping cart and wheeled it into the school.

With the security standards of today, it may seem rather hard to believe that two people could bring guns and explosives into a school so easily, but at the time there was nothing stopping these misanthropic terrorists from doing so. They were actually greeted by the school receptionist, who saw some of their weaponry in plain sight yet assumed that there must be a rational reason for it. Wyoming was hunting country, after all, and back in the 1980s seeing someone waltzing around with a shotgun was not that unusual. So even though the couple was armed to the teeth, the receptionist still drawled out her customary, "How can I help you?"

But while the stash of weapons they were wheeling around had failed to trigger any alarm bells for the laid-back Wyoming woman, David's response to her inquiry certainly did. He screamed out, "This is a revolution!" You can imagine this poor school clerk's confusion as she stared down this monster and mumbled, "I beg your pardon?" David made everything clear in his next statement as he commanded, "This school is being taken hostage! Don't push any alarms, answer any phones, or call for help! We are very serious!"

He then motioned toward the shopping cart, revealing that he was attached to it by wires, and added, "I have guns and this is a bomb!" David was wired to the bomb with what experts call a "dead man switch". This meant that the bomb would go off if David was killed.

He then ordered the stunned receptionist to disconnect the main phone lines so that no one could call out from the school. Keep in mind that this was 1986 Wyoming; nobody had cell phones, so the landline was really the only means of communication outside of the school.

Taking the receptionist with them, David and Dorra gathered a few additional hostages as they roamed the school's halls, then barged into a classroom full of children and began to set up shop. Teacher Jean Mitchel was just getting ready to teach her excited pupils about one of their favorite subjects—dinosaurs. But instead of being able to regale her students with tales of the mighty T-Rex, she was now forced to confront a tall, shabbily dressed man wheeling a shopping cart full of explosives into her classroom.

Dorra and the hostages poured into the room behind him, and before this startled teacher and her curious students could even process what was happening, David began shouting out his demands as he brandished several weapons in front of them. Making one of the hostages his "spokesperson", David ordered him to go to one of the phones that were still operating to alert the authorities and demand two million dollars for each of his hostages.

As this errand was being carried out, the impatient and rambunctious youngsters soon became too much for even the supreme intellect of David Young to handle. Hoping to prevent the hyperactive students from causing the already agitated madman to set off the bomb, one of the teachers—with David's permission, of course—had the idea to lay tape down on the carpet in a square around David and the bomb. This was to be the boundary separating him from the kids, so that they didn't inadvertently bump into him. This tactic seemed to work, and after the square was established, the children made sure they kept outside of the tape.

However, although this crisis was averted, another one followed close on its heels. Strong fumes from the bomb began making several of the students sick, and in order to mitigate this malady, the teachers prevailed upon David to allow them to open the windows. David, also feeling the effects of the fumes, readily agreed. Once all of the windows in the classroom were opened, the teachers and students began to pray together for a safe resolution to the crisis.

Although he didn't stop them, David was visibly disturbed by their prayers. He decided to relinquish control of the "dead man switch" of his bomb to Dorra so he could go to the bathroom. This proved to be a bad move, since Dorra was even more agitated and erratic than he was. When the children's incessant talking got to grating on her nerves, she began to gesture wildly for them to be quiet—and in her agitation, Dorra managed to inadvertently set off the bomb!

Those who were there remember the next few moments as being completely surreal, with the roar of flames from the explosive material engulfing the entire classroom. Fortunately, the open windows gave the kids an easy means of escape, and many of them began to climb out and drop down onto the lawn outside. David Young, meanwhile, hearing the explosion, decided to go ahead and take his own life. He was later found dead from a self-inflicted gunshot wound.

Miraculously, Dorra and David were the only casualties; all of their hostages survived. Later on, several of the children would claim that they had seen angels hovering near the ceiling immediately before and after the explosion. They believed that these angels had shielded them from the blast. The Cokeville Sheriff also claimed to have had a kind of divine encounter: While he was frantically trying to rescue the victims, he heard a reassuring voice tell him that everything was going to be okay.

Besides these incredible testimonials, this case actually has some physical evidence as well, in the form of a startling crime scene photo taken shortly after the explosion. This picture, which has long since traveled the paranormal circuit, does indeed seem to depict the shadow of a giant winged figure standing watch over the classroom. Did angels protect Cokeville Elementary during its time of crisis? It's fascinating to think about—but perhaps we will never know.

World War One's Angels of Mons

When it was fought a century ago, the First World War was said to be the "war to end all wars" due to its sheer brutality and unprecedented mechanized slaughter. (Unfortunately, this appellation proved to be mistaken; it not only didn't end all wars, it didn't even prevent the devastating conflagration known as World War Two, which still stands as one of the most brutal conflicts humanity has ever had to endure.) All of Western Europe had been converted into battlefields of trenches in which machine guns and artillery butchered troops in the thousands as they tried to advance a few feet further. Much of the war was a completely senseless and intractable quagmire. If there was ever a crisis that needed some angelic intervention, the bloody, death-filled trenches of World War One certainly qualified.

It was still early in the war, on August 26, 1914, when the British General Horace Smith-Dorrien issued a command to his small but well-equipped unit. He ordered his troops to charge the Germans holed up in what used to be the Belgian city of Le Cateau. Used to be, because with all of the ground dug up into trenches and machine gun installations stretching across the landscape as far as the eye could see, this battle zone could hardly be said to resemble a city any longer. It was in this deadly environment that this small British band was tasked with standing up to the German advance.

They were trying their best to push the Germans back, but were being consistently mowed down by German machine gun fire. Their casualties quickly spiked to 7,812 without much progress being made. The situation was going from bad to worse, and when the group reached the Belgian city of Mons it was finally acknowledged that a strategic retreat would have to be made. But the British soldiers were now nearly surrounded on all sides, and any withdraw at this point put them at risk of complete annihilation by their German pursuers.

During this crisis of the highest order, several of the British troops—and even some Germans—allegedly saw angelic apparitions protecting the retreating Brits. One of the most popular accounts recorded the sighing of the Angel of the Lord, dressed all in white, atop a white horse charging at the Germans with a flaming sword to prevent them from pursuing the British.

Others claimed to have seen whole battalions of angels blocking or even actively engaging the German advance. Most famously, however, apparitions dressed like archers from the British medieval period were seen shooting phantom arrows at the Germans. It is not entirely clear what effect these ghostly arrows had, but the entities became known as the "Bowmen of Mons" and were regarded as a direct divine intervention sent to those desperate troops in their greatest time of need.

Angels as Messengers

The holy books of Judaism, Christianity, and Islam are all three filled with numerous accounts of angels serving as divine messengers. The very beginning of the Christian narrative has the angel Gabriel informing the Virgin Mary that she is going to carry the Christ child. And according to adherents of Islam, this very same Gabriel imparted the ultimate message of God's final revelation to the prophet Muhammad. The Jewish Torah, the foundation of both Christianity and Islam, is also filled with accounts of God using his angels as messengers.

As beings somewhere between God and man, angels seem to be the perfect heralds to humanity. In fact, the Greek root of the word angel, "*angelo*", actually means "messenger". In this chapter, you will find accounts of this angelic mission continuing to this very day.

A Vietnam Vet's Angelic Message of Peace, Protection, and Deliverance

The Vietnam War was a dreadful conflict by any stretch of the imagination, and the quagmire began long before American troops ever touched Vietnamese soil. The roots of the struggle can be traced back to World War Two, when a weakened and defeated France lost control of its colonial possessions in Indochina. Metropolitan France having been overrun by Nazi Germany, the Nazis' Asian ally Japan took the opportunity to annex French holdings which included modern-day Cambodia, Laos, and Vietnam.

After World War Two ended in defeat for the Japanese, the French desperately attempted to reassert control over their far-flung former colonies. But Vietnam was fast slipping from their grasp, and as in many parts of the postwar world, communist activists seized popular anticolonial sentiment for their own ends. Many Vietnamese joined the communist cause in order to shake off the yoke of French domination.

At this point the French struggle against the Vietnamese became more than an isolated case of old-fashioned colonial conquest. Now it was a struggle against a collectivist ideology that was growing worldwide. As such, the entire communist world lent its support—both material and moral—to the fight in Southeast Asia. The French struggled against this implacable foe for over a decade before a United States administration increasingly alarmed about the spread of communism decided to take action.

American intervention led to yet another decade of protracted struggle. By this point French colonialism had been rejected, and Vietnam was already guaranteed independence whether it was communist or not. The conflict had now morphed into the U.S.-backed nationalist South against the communist North. And in February of 1970, American soldier Gary Sanders was deployed right into the middle of this growing storm.

On the very day of his arrival, the helicopter carrying him onto the battlefield was overwhelmed by heavy artillery fire and forced to make an impromptu landing. Only once the enemy had been fought off could Gary and his fellow troops continue onward to their destination. Arriving at the base, Gary was assigned to a security detail and became part of a regular night watch outfit. While he was making his rounds one night, an angelic messenger came to visit him.

To his disbelief, as he stared out into the darkness at what had been an empty rice paddy, a flash of illumination revealed a giant winged figure standing in the field. Gary's mind couldn't make sense of what he was seeing, but his training already had him grabbing his gun and aiming at the apparition. Fortunately, before Gary could pull the trigger, the angel instructed him, "Put it down Gary. You have nothing to fear."

As soon as the angel said these words, feelings of peace and calm washed through him, and he truly did feel his fear subside as he lowered the weapon. The figure then smiled gently at him and said, "Gary, I'm here to tell you that you have nothing to fear or worry about. You will be protected and looked after. You still have many things to do in life." According to Gary, after this message of divine reassurance had been delivered, the being simply waved its hand at him and disappeared.

An Angelic Message of Marital Reconciliation

Dave Brown had been married to Sandy for 20 years, and he felt that the union had been a happy one—but he couldn't have been more mistaken. Although Dave was a successful businessman, he had been so consumed with his work and his out-of-town business trips that he had neglected to shower his wife and kids with the attention that they needed. Even though it was obvious to everyone else that his affection-starved wife had reached a breaking point, Dave was completely unaware of the situation that was about to unfold.

Then one night while he was up late balancing the books, Sandy barged into his study to deliver an ultimatum. She informed him in no uncertain terms, "Dave, I'm leaving you. I'm going to take the kids and stay at my mother's house for a few days to think things out. If you want me to come back, you are going to have to change your ways." Dave couldn't believe what he was hearing. He just stared in absolute shock as she shut the door behind her.

Dave was a real perfectionist, and he thought that he had his whole life mapped out and under control. To now hear that the most important part of his life was unraveling was too much to bear. But he wasn't immediately moved to make things right with his wife. Instead, he became angry at what was happening to him. His mind screamed, "She's leaving me?!? She's leaving me?!?" The thought that Sandy would unilaterally disrupt his carefully laid-out plans infuriated him to no end.

Dave himself had come from a broken home, with a father who was never around, and he carried a considerable amount of anger on account of this. For the most part he had been able to channel this aggression into positive things such as work. But now that this singular focus on his job had backfired, the anger came back to him like a flood. After Sandy left, he reached for the bottle of vodka that he kept hidden in his desk drawer and began to take swig after swig of the hard liquor.

As he downed the vodka he stumbled through the house like a madman, gathering every picture of Sandy and personal memento of married life so he could destroy them all. He threw pictures against the wall or threw them to the floor and violently stomped on them with his feet. Finally he found a vase of flowers that he had just gotten Sandy to commemorate their 20th wedding anniversary. Completely consumed with rage, and with her words of "I'm leaving you" still reverberating in his mind, he picked up the vase and crushed it with his bare hands.

Predictably, the shards of broken pottery cut deep into his skin. The physical pain of his punctured palm managed to trigger the deep sadness his rage had temporarily obscured, and Dave immediately fell to his knees and wept as he cradled his bleeding hand. In his despair, he noticed one of the pottery shards next to him. It was particularly sharp, and jagged. He picked it up, and looking at his upturned left arm, he decided that he was going to end it all right there by slashing his wrist.

But just as he was getting ready to do it, he heard a voice command him, "Stop!" Seeing light out of the corner of his eye, Dave turned toward the corner of the room and saw a beautiful winged angel staring back at him. As he watched in shock, being repeated once again, "Stop!' Dave dropped the broken shard and stared in fear at the apparition before him.

The angel then sought to comfort him. "Dave, do not be afraid. I was sent here to stop you from doing something you would regret." Dave managed to mumble, "Regret?" The angel nodded. "Yes—you were about to take your own life, and that would have been a terrible tragedy." The angel then continued, "Don't forfeit this life God has given you. Go to your wife and tell her that you love her."

Then there was a flash and the being simply vanished before his eyes as if it had never been there to begin with. The message was simple in scope, but Dave immediately understood what he needed to do, and seeing the angel gave him the confidence that he needed to do it. He stood up and marched to the door, now determined to plead his case to his wife, telling her he loved her more than anything in this world and would do anything to keep her at his side.

But before he could even place his hand on the doorknob, the knob turned by itself and the door began to open. For a moment Dave wondered if the angelic visitor was returning. At least this time it had been thoughtful enough to use the door! But it wasn't an angel, at least not of the celestial kind: It was Sandy. As he stepped backward from the opening door, his wife stepped over the threshold and fell right into his arms.

She then looked up at him with an awestruck face as she somberly informed him, "Dave, you are never going to believe this, but I saw an angel, and he told me you needed me and that I should come back." This particular angel had apparently been very busy that night! This angelic messenger had managed to bring to people on the verge of complete perdition back from the brink with his message of unity and reconciliation. At any rate, this is a tale well worth believing!

Archangel Michael's Message for Little Francoise

Her name was Francoise de Sery, and she was just a girl of 13, but on that cold morning in early February, 1942, she felt old beyond her years. The pressure of living in Nazi-occupied France and her father's recent detention by the Gestapo had filled this innocent child's heart with worry and fear. Her whole world had been turned upside down, and there didn't seem to be any relief in sight.

But even in this atmosphere of severe distress, life went on. People still went to work, and children still went to school—which is precisely what little Francoise was attempting to do when she had an intervention of the angelic kind. On her way to school, an impeccably well-dressed man approached her and imparted a simple yet profound message, telling her, "*Francoise, ton pere sera la pour dejeuner.*"— "Francoise, your father is coming home for lunch."

Francoise's eyes opened wide and she was immediately flooded with emotion. Hearing that her beloved father would soon be coming home was more than she could ever have hoped for. But at the same time, there was fear here too. Who was this man? And how did he know about her father? In the paranoid world of occupied France, where people talked low and quiet out of fear of the wrong person hearing their conversation, to hear such incredible news boldly proclaimed was highly unusual.

Her besieged mind had to consider that the whole thing might be a ruse. What if this man was playing a trick on her? Perhaps he was even one of the Nazis who had interrogated her father, and he had tracked her down and was trying to get her hopes up in an effort to get her to crack and divulge information. But as she looked upon the kind countenance of this stranger, all of these fears were cast aside, and she knew that there was no way that this person was plotting anything of the kind.

When he said that her father would be home, she believed it with all her heart. She also found the man strangely familiar; she somehow knew that she had seen him before. Suddenly it occurred to her that she had just had a dream in which she saw this very same figure telling her that her father would be coming home soon. During her dream, she had gotten the strong impression that the being was the Archangel Michael. As she

36

stared in awe at what she now believed to be an angel standing right in front of her, the being turned and crossed the street.

A bus then turned the corner and blocked Francoise's line of sight. After it passed, the man/angel she had encountered had completely vanished. It was broad daylight, there wasn't anywhere he could have gone, but he had disappeared without a trace. To Francoise, it seemed that this celestial visitor had simply delivered his intended message and then returned from whence he had come.

She couldn't shake the experience from her mind even after she arrived at school. She kept hearing the angel's words that her father was coming back. When she headed home for lunch as she always did and ran into the house to tell her startled mother the news, the despondent woman did not believe her at first. But Francoise didn't have to wait long for confirmation of the angel's prediction. Just seconds later, the door to the family home creaked open and there was her dad standing right there in front of them.

He looked like he hadn't slept in days, but besides being a bit rough around the edges, he was relatively unharmed. The Nazis had subjected him to a lengthy interrogation, but after determining that he didn't have any valuable intel to give, they had turned him loose and ordered him to go home. Archangel Michael's message of deliverance was just what little Francois needed during her hour of despair.

Angels to the Rescue

Sometimes life throws up emergencies so grave that it seems only an angel from heaven could possibly lead us out of the danger we are in. And in the following accounts, according to those who lived through them, this is precisely what happened!

Cheyenne McKee Saved by the Angelic Host

Cheyenne was never a religious or even particularly spiritual person growing up. Her parents had never mentioned God or angels, and she'd never really thought about such things either. But as one anonymous soldier stuck in a hole in the ground with bullets raining down on top of him put it long ago, "there are no atheists in foxholes." In other words, we all tend to grasp for spiritual help when we are in serious need of a rescue.

And this was precisely the case with Cheyenne. She was on what was so far a very happy and fulfilling hiking trip with her fiancé Dave when in a split second her joy turned to absolute horror. Her fiancé, who was an expert climber, was helping her over a ledge on a rock face they were ascending when he abruptly slipped, lost his footing, and fell off the side of the cliff.

The deadly event took a matter of seconds, but Cheyenne watched Dave begin to slide as if in slow motion. He looked her right in the eyes as he fell backwards. When Dave landed down below, he hit head first, and there was no question that he died instantly on impact. Cheyenne let out anguished screams for her beloved boyfriend—until her sorrow was superseded by the realization that she too was in incredible danger.

She found herself unable to move up or down on the sheer cliff that she clung to, and she knew that there was a good chance she would meet the same fate as her fiancé, plummeting down to her death on the rocks below. And so she cried out in full faith to the deity that she never even knew she believed in. In her agonized terror, she screamed, "Oh God—please! Please help me!" Her cries for help seemed to tap into something deep inside of her, and she felt as if she was now somehow connected directly to the divine.

And as if in response, she immediately began to see angels all around her. They hovered in formation in the air surrounding her position on the rock wall as if they were forming a protective barrier to make sure she didn't slip and fall. As we've established, Cheyenne was not a religious person, but curiously enough, a piece of unfamiliar scripture inexplicably popped into her mind. It was a passage from the book of Isaiah.

As she witnessed the supernatural forces at work around her, she could hear it echoing through her mind: "But they that wait upon the Lord shall renew their strength; they shall mount up with wings as eagles." And indeed, as if she had suddenly grown a pair of eagle's wings herself, the next thing she knew she was 300 feet further down the slick rock wall. She does not remember climbing down; it was as if she had been miraculously transported there.

But even with this divine assistance, she was still about 100 feet from the bottom and still very much in danger of sliding the rest of the way down. And that's when it happened—her worst fear was realized when, just like her fiancé before her, she slipped, lost her footing and began to slide uncontrollably down the rock face. Was her previous show of faith and the appearance of the angels all for naught? Why would they render aid only to abandon her at this critical moment? What kind of cosmic cruelty was this?

But even as she fell, she could sense that invisible hands were somehow guiding her along, and before she reached the bottom she slowly (and inexplicably) slid to a stop. She should have plummeted to her death, but instead she made a completely controlled landing. With freedom now just a few feet below her, she was easily able to jump down and escape. She felt that the angelic host she had witnessed had personally come to her rescue and escorted her off the cliff.

Cheyenne rushed to call emergency services, and a rescue team was dispatched to search for her fiancé. When they found him, her worst fear was confirmed: her fiancé Dave was indeed already dead. But despite this tragic loss, Cheyenne would consider her heartfelt prayers for rescue as she clung to that impossible rock face to have been answered.

The Mysterious Case of the Angel Staircase

When it comes to angel lore, this one is an absolute legend. And although it doesn't involve a dramatic physical rescue of someone whose life was in danger, a church facing hard times was rescued all the same. The story begins all the way back in 1852 when seven nuns from the order of the Sisters of Loretto answered a call for the establishment of a new ministry in the American Southwest and set out to build a school for the region's underprivileged youth.

They left Kentucky for Santa Fe, New Mexico, which was still just a U.S. territory at the time. The trip was long and arduous, and one of the nuns fell sick with cholera along the way and had to turn back. The remaining six persevered, but at one point it seemed that disaster was about to overcome them all when a group of hostile Native Americans surrounded their convoy and began threatening them.

The nuns started praying, and miraculously the Native Americans suddenly turned around and sped off. It was as if something had frightened them off. What was it that had so terrified these usually fearless warriors? Did some sort of angelic protector answer the nuns' prayer?

Tragedy soon struck the women again when another member of their group came down with cholera and died. Now down to just five members, this group of brave nuns continued on their journey. When they finally arrived, they found Santa Fe to be a hopelessly backward patchwork of Hispanic and Native American families, most of whom were unable to read or write. The nuns knew that the school they were planning to build would be a much-needed staple of this community.

Bishop Jean-Baptiste Lamy had a chapel constructed in 1872. When the sisters arrived on the scene they saw its many buttresses, spires, and beautiful stained-glass windows and believed that it was a great building in which to begin their ministry. There was only problem: It was a two-story building with no way of reaching the top floor except the ladders used by priests. Ladders, however, just wouldn't do for nuns wearing long dresses.

So the sisters began looking into getting a proper staircase built. But the builders they brought in all took one look at the chapel's floor plan and stated that it would be impossible to create a usable staircase in such a small amount of space. Fearing that all of their carefully conceived plans would come to naught over something as trivial as a staircase, the nuns began to pray for someone to come to their rescue.

The answer to their prayers arrived in the form of a bearded man wearing weather-beaten clothing and looking altogether rough around the edges. The stranger rode up to the chapel on a donkey and offered his services. He said that his name was Joseph, and although he had only the most basic of carpentry tools with him, he assured the sisters that he could indeed build them their staircase.

The man set about his work in complete secrecy, never asking any questions and never asking for any help. And upon completion of the project, he left the scene quietly without even asking for any payment. He left an exquisite spiral staircase stretching from the bottom to the top of the chapel, seeming to defy gravity in its spiraling climb to the heavens.

Architects and engineers have long been baffled as to how the staircase can be stable without any centralized support mechanisms. Based upon their educated observations, the staircase should not be structurally sound. And yet it was used for over 100 years without any problems whatsoever. In fact, it is still standing; the only change has been the addition of a railing to reassure those who were made a little queasy by the steep drop!

Many have since speculated that the mysterious stranger who built this intricate masterpiece for free must have been an angel laboring on behalf of God himself. Others have suggested that the old master carpenter was actually Christ's father Joseph, returning to show off his expertise one more time. At any rate, when the nuns needed to be rescued, they weren't disappointed.

Angels Come to Belinda's Rescue

Full-time laboratory pathologist and part-time paranormal enthusiast Belinda Bevins claims to have experienced several forms of divine intervention over the past 25 years. These include three events in which angels have really seemed to come to her rescue. The first occurred at a church gathering in Kentucky. It was a lazy summer day, and her church's youth program had taken the kids to swim in a nearby river.

Belinda loved the water, and was floating on her back and relaxing. She soon lost track of her position and was carried away from the other church members by the powerful current. And not only was she moving rapidly away from everyone else, the water was threatening to push her to the bottom! As she struggled to keep her head above water, she realized that she was about to drown.

Instead of panic, however, a sense of peace came over her, and she felt prepared to meet her fate. But apparently an angelic intercessor wasn't ready to let Belinda make that journey to heaven just yet. Somehow, just when she thought she was done for, she felt something pick her up by her bathing suit, lift her head above water, and carry her all the way to the other side of the river, where it placed her back down in calm, shallow waters. She is absolutely convinced that angels rescued her on that day when no one else could.

The next major angelic event to occur in Belinda's life happened when she was 23 and a friend was giving her a ride to the university laboratory where she was studying. Her friend suddenly lost control of the car, sending them straight for the headlights of another vehicle at a high rate of speed. Just like she had during her brush with death in the river as a child, Belinda felt convinced that she was on her way to heaven. But once again, an angel came to the rescue, taking control of the car, steering it away from danger and parking it safely on the side of the road. There was no explanation of how the car managed to avoid the collision, but both young women were spared what would most likely have been a lethal accident.

But Belinda's most powerful angel rescue was still to come. The incident occurred just few years later, when she was 29 and working in a bio-lab researching stem cell cultures. She was placing a Petri dish under a microscope when the facility seemed to disappear around her and she was transported into a majestic Greco-Roman styled amphitheater.

She looked up to see a being that she intuitively knew to be the Archangel Gabriel. Gabriel was dressed in fine white raiment that seemed to let off an unearthly light and came carrying a trumpet, just as described in the Bible. Belinda watched quietly as he put the trumpet to his lips and let loose a blast that seemed to contain a full orchestra in one single note. Gabriel then turned to Belinda and revealed to her why she had been rescued so many times.

The angel told her that she was destined to help a great many people before she left this world. A part of her wondered if this would have something to do with her research in medicine. Was she going to find a cure for a deadly disease? Would she save millions of lives as a result? But besides the more conventional explanations as to how she might help others, she knew that the hope the angels placed on her was even bigger than that.

From the message Gabriel delivered to her, it was clear that she was to help others not only physically, but also spiritually. The angels wanted her to help humanity understand just how much God loves us, and how important we are to him. Shortly after this was communicated, Belinda was instantly back in the lab as if it had all been some kind of bizarre daydream.

But in her heart of hearts, Belinda Bevins knew that there was no way that she had dreamed all of this up. It was all too real. As in her two previous encounters, the angels had come at just the right time in her life. And even though she wasn't rescued from any immediate physical calamity in this third interaction with angels, she believed that through the revelation of their words she had once again been delivered by them all the same.

Angels as Guides to the Other Side

It goes without saying that death is the biggest transition we will ever have to make. And if angels are indeed there to help and guide us along, it should come as no surprise that the angelic host would have a role in shepherding us over to the other side. Here in this chapter we will discuss some of the finer details of the many accounts of angelic involvement with near death experiences, the final goodbyes of our deceased loved ones, and in helping us conquer own fear of that spiritual journey.

Have a Drink on Me and my Angel Buddies

It sounds comical, and perhaps contradictory to most religious sensibilities, to imagine angels making that great trip from Heaven just to visit folks drinking and living it up at a local bar. But if you believe the account handed down to us by a young Irishman named Braedon Jones, this is precisely what happened! The events allegedly occurred shortly after the death of Braedon's father, Corey.

Corey's demise was not unexpected; he was 78, and his wife had already passed a few months before. But it was a particularly hard blow for Braedon to lose his elderly father so close on the heels of his mother. And it was especially hard considering his father's condition just before he died. His overall physical health didn't raise any particular alarm bells, but his mental state was quite distressing for those that were around him.

He was completely consumed with grief for his beloved wife and seemed to be refusing to go on without her. And as is often said, Corey appears to have died of a broken heart. According to his other son, Aiden, it was hard to get his father out of the house during his last few months of life. The one time of day he could always do so was during the early afternoon hours, when he could convince him to come out to the neighborhood bar.

Here he could ease his father's tension with a few drinks and temporarily restore him to his jolly, conversational old self. Aidan felt bad that alcohol was the only way he could get his father to open up to him, but it was the only thing that worked on his deep melancholy. And even in the bar, when his thoughts returned to his dearly departed wife, Corey would instantly sink back into the depths of despair.

One day however, when the subject came up, he didn't sink into depression immediately. Instead, he had some very serious words of advice for his son. While they were discussing how suddenly Mrs. Jones had died, Corey suddenly offered the matter-of-fact advice with a look of profound thoughtfulness: "Listen son, don't worry or feel too bad when I go. The angels will take care of me just like they're taking care of your mom."

Braedon, who was also present, couldn't figure out why such a thought would suddenly pop into the elderly man's head in the middle of a father-and-son drinking session. He had never talked much about angels, let alone asserted that they care for us either here or on the other side. But now he suddenly seemed quite convinced of this. However, upon being pressed to elaborate on this random revelation, Corey declined. He just insisted that Braedon, Aiden and their two sisters not worry about him.

But what really perked Corey up out of his previous gloom was telling his sons how he wished his funeral to be carried out! It seemed odd indeed that a man who was deeply depressed would only get into a good mood when discussing his own funeral, but this was precisely how it happened. No matter how much his children tried to change the subject, the old man would always go back to funeral arrangements. And more than anything else, Corey wanted his friends and family to have a good time.

There at the local tavern, he informed his sons that he wanted all of those in attendance not to mourn, but rather to celebrate life! And being the drinker that he was, Corey specifically asked that a glass be raised in his honor right over his casket! Braedon tried to take such remarks with good humor, but when his dad passed away a few months later, thinking about Corey's last requests only made him sad.

But then as he was going through some of his belongings, he found an envelope. Inside was about 500 dollars in cash and a handwritten note. Scrawled on the piece of paper were his dad's specific instructions to spend the 500 bucks on booze for his funeral! Wishing to abide by his father's wishes no matter how eccentric and colorful, Braedon dutifully tucked the money away and prepared for the funeral.

At the conclusion of the service, and to the barely contained amusement of those in attendance, Braedon stood up and announced that the reception would be held at the nearby pub—and the drinks came courtesy of his dad's post-mortem generosity! Braedon describes the affair as a happy and joyous get-together of friends and family, just as his father had wished. He was glad to be able to fulfill Corey's last request, but as the night wore on sadness started to grip him once again.

Suddenly wishing to be alone, he excused himself from the tavern's function room where everyone was gathered and took a seat at the empty bar on the other side of the establishment. As he stared down at that somber bar, the realization that he would never see either of his parents again took hold of him. But just as he felt that he was about to break his father's commandment to "be happy" during his funeral and burst into uncontrollable tears on that barstool, something compelled him to turn his head and look out the window.

He could see a group of people standing outside in the distance looking in his direction. Braedon's first reaction to being stared at by these figures was a quite understandable, "Huh? What are they looking at?" But as he squinted his eyes and looked closer, something seemed unusual about his stargazing admirers. Their faces seemed to emanate some kind of radiant light. As he focused in, Braedon could just make out that they were absolutely beaming at him, smiling with the most loving and adoring of smiles.

They simply radiated serenity, and they passed on these peaceful feelings to him as he watched them. There were four entities standing in the distance, and when he paid closer attention to the middle pair he realized that he was looking at none other than his deceased mother and father! As for the beings that flanked them on either side, he could only assume they were angels!

Just as his father had foretold, these angelic beings were apparently taking care of his parents on the other side! As soon as Braedon was given this revelation, the radiant figures of his parents and their personal angelic attendants disappeared in a flash. But even after their departure, this fleeting glimpse was more than enough to reassure Braedon that everything was going to be alright.

Jesse Duplantis and His Close Encounters of the God Kind

Jesse Duplantis is a beloved minister from Southern Louisiana with an easy smile and an even easier ability to crack gut-busting jokes in the middle of his sermons. He usually keeps the subject matter light and to the point, and from his preaching you might never guess the heavy things that he claims to have gone through. In particular, he claims that after a period of intense prayer several years ago, an angel came down and escorted him to heaven.

However, this was not the first time that Rev. Duplantis claims to have seen an angel. He contends that the encounters began several years before when he woke up shortly after midnight to find a giant angel standing at the foot of his bed. According to Rev. Duplantis, this angel was sent during a time of great stress in his life when he was uncertain just where to take his ministry. This angel had a simple message, however, informing him, "I have been sent by the Lord. You are under much stress, and the Lord sent me to tell you to sleep."

Rev. Duplantis was too awestruck by the being to offer much of an argument, but as important as sleep was for the overworked preacher, this experience seemed rather anticlimactic. What supposedly happened to Rev. Duplantis when he again encountered an angel in August of 1988 would be nothing of the kind. During that hot August, he was doing the rounds at a series of summer revival services in Magnolia, Arkansas, as a visiting guest speaker.

When he wasn't preaching, Rev. Duplantis was usually holed up in a motel without much else to do. But one day he was invited to eat lunch with a local pastor prior to an afternoon service. Right before the appointment, Rev. Duplantis started to feel rather peculiar. He just had this strange, unshakeable feeling that something highly unusual was about to occur. This feeling stayed with him throughout his lunch with the minister, and eventually Rev. Duplantis felt so uncomfortable that he had to excuse himself.

He told his host, "I don't mean to be rude, but I have to go back to the motel. Something is up. I just don't know what."

Startled, his colleague asked, "Are you sick?"

Rev. Duplantis assured the man, "No, nothing is wrong. I just… have to get back to my room. I'm sorry. Please excuse me."

Rev. Duplantis then left the restaurant and went straight to his motel room, where he immediately kneeled down and began to pray. As soon as he began praying, he felt like he was being "pulled up out of the room", right through the walls and ceiling of the motel.

The next thing he knew, Rev. Duplantis found himself in a vehicle that he describes as a kind of "cable car"—except without the cable—hurtling at terrific speed up through the atmosphere. Looking around, he saw that there was another passenger on board: the same angel who'd told him to get some sleep. This time, the laconic angel simply grinned at him and informed him, "You have an appointment with the Lord God Jehovah." Then the vehicle stopped, the door opened, and as Rev. Duplantis looked outside of the craft, he realized that he was in heaven.

Whether the vehicle was inter-dimensional in nature or a standard-fare "chariot of fire" is hard to say, but as Rev. Duplantis puts it, "Heaven must not be too far away. I didn't seem as if I had gone out of our galaxy. Of course, I'm not an astronomer, so I really don't know for sure." At any rate, the angel then became a kind of heavenly tour guide and began to show him around. He was amazed to find that heaven had many of the things we value here on earth, including mountains, rivers, and flowers.

As Rev. Duplantis traversed heaven, the similarities between beautiful things from the realm of the living and the afterlife began to puzzle him—so much so that he questioned it. In response he was informed, "Jesse, the earth is God's creation. His taste there is his taste here." Basically, beautiful mountains, rivers, and flowers are in heaven simply because God wants them to be there!

Rev. Duplantis then began to notice several other people arriving in heaven just like he had. As he gazed upon these arrivals, Rev. Duplantis was made to realize that these were people who had died and crossed over to the other side. Some of them seemed physically weak and could barely even walk. The angel explained that it was the spiritual weakness of these individuals that was troubling them. Motioning toward the struggling souls, the angel remarked, "Some of them did not live the life they should have. They believe in God and love Jesus, but they didn't live to their fullest potential." Rev. Duplantis claims that these weak newcomers were given fruit to eat, and once they ate it, they were imbued with renewed strength and were able to continue their progress.

After observing this, Rev. Duplantis continued on what was truly a grand tour of heaven. He claims to have been introduced firsthand to biblical patriarchs such as Abraham and New Testament church leaders like the Apostle Paul. He was then taken to have an audience with Christ himself, who was actively preaching to the souls in heaven just like he did on Earth. According to Rev. Duplantis, even in heaven there is much that we can still learn, and spiritual advancement is an active and ongoing process.

As his trip came to a close, the angel took Rev. Duplantis to the throne room of God. Rev. As they got closer and closer, he began to see more and more people gathered around ready to seek audience with the most-high. But as he neared God himself, he began to feel increasingly weaker, much like those new arrivals to heaven who could barely stagger out of their "chariots". As a remedy, Rev. Duplantis claims, he was beckoned to eat the same fruit that the angels had given the other spiritually famished individuals. This imbued him with enough strength and power to go on, and thus bolstered, he finally made his way directly in front of God.

The room itself was huge, and God was surrounded by angels, some of them flying around him in circles. Rev. Duplantis felt weak from the brilliant light emanating from all directions, and so one of the angels gave him (yep, you guessed it) another piece of heavenly fruit to eat so he could withstand its brilliance a little while longer. Nevertheless, the Rev. Duplantis tour of heaven soon came to a close, and he was transported back to his motel room.

It's undeniably tempting to openly ridicule such a fantastic story. Even many of the most committed Christians would perceive this tale of walking with angels, patriarchs, apostles, and even Christ and God himself as just too farfetched to believe. Others, on the other hand, would say that the story is so bizarre that Rev. Duplantis could hardly have made it up!

Whatever the truth may be, for his part Rev. Duplantis has stuck by his account of this angelic joyride to the other side for several decades now, and seems primed to do so for the foreseeable future as well. He first went public with his account in 1988 in his now infamous book *Close Encounters of the God Kind*, and he holds firm on his encounter to this very day.

U.S. Senator Vetoes an Angel's Invitation to the Other Side

It certainly sounds like a headline from a tabloid news article, but this tale of angelic stewardship to the great beyond didn't come from any questionable "source"—it came straight from the senator himself. Back in 2012, Senator Mark Kirk of Illinois had a massive stroke. He was rushed to the hospital, where physicians worked around the clock to stabilize him. They thought that they had succeeded, but then the senator began to slip away once again.

Senator Kirk somehow knew that his life essence was leaving him. As he describes it, "A thing just went off in my head and I knew that this was the end." And although the senator wasn't too happy about that fact, he wasn't fearful either. Like so many others who have been in the presence of the divine, he experienced a sense of profound peace flooding over him. And at precisely that moment, he saw three angels standing at the foot of his bed.

Just to be clear, these angels weren't actually attending physicians, nurses, physical therapists, or some other kind of misidentified medical worker—of this the senator is certain. According to Senator Kirk, there should have been no one else in his room at that hour. And besides—since when do nurses glow in the dark?!? As the senator describes it, these angelic beings were absolutely radiating light, and it was this light, Senator Kirk realized, that was also instilling him with his profound sense of peace, love and acceptance.

Even so, he wasn't quite ready to let go. And when one of the angels opened its mouth to ask him point blank, "Would you like to come with us?" Senator Kirk overruled the celestial entity, bluntly informing it, "No, I'll hold off." Senator Kirk apparently had some important legislation ahead of him, and he couldn't allow even death to stand in his way. As a matter of fact, after this incredible event transpired, he made sure that he returned to Congress for its very next session!

When the senator informed the angel of his desire to stay on this plane of existence, it seemed to respect his choice. Then it abruptly winked out of existence! Now, maybe at this point you're shaking your head and thinking, "Gee, if I knew it was that easy to cheat death, I never would have bought a life insurance policy!" But as zany as the senator's story sounds, he is absolutely convinced that it really happened.

Apparently, nothing was going to get in the way of this senator's closing remarks! No matter how much his winged watchers wanted to take him over to the great beyond, Senator Kirk was more than ready to veto their proposal. So, let that be a lesson to the rest of you: If you're nearing the end and the Angel of Death comes calling, just take one from the senator's playbook and filibuster that grim reaper right back to the abyss!

Conclusion

Are there really invisible angels flitting about, flying back and forth, waiting to swoop down and render aid? To many in the modern world, the idea is absurd. Yet whether we admit it or not, even those of us who are skeptics still can't help but feel a deep affinity for the idea of these supposed winged guardians. We would all like to have some sort of powerful protector looking out for us.

So it really is no wonder that even in our highly advanced, technological society, we find ourselves longing for our winged brethren just as much as we did back in the dark ages. Because as much as humanity has learned, there is still quite a bit that we don't know—and it frightens us. It is due to this latent fear of the dark that we seek the light. Whether the stories presented here are true, imagined, or perhaps a mixture of both, they present that real desire that all of us have for powerful friends, guardians, and guides.

In this troubled world we could all use that extra guiding hand to steady us on our path. We could all use that hidden friend and guardian during our times of crisis and our hours of darkness. And as long as humanity feels at least somewhat inadequate in dealing with the uncertainty of life, that longing will remain. And as long as that need exists, you can almost certainly guarantee that we will continue to appeal to our better angels.

Further Readings

Here at the end let's take the time to explore some of the materials and resources that helped to make this book possible. There are many books, articles, and documentaries on the subject of angels. In order to understand this complex subject clearly, you need to examine it from many different angles (no, that's not a typo; angels have many different angles). So feel free to explore all of the great resources listed below in your own personal search for the angelic.

***Where Angels Walk: True Stories of Heavenly Visitors*. Joan Wester Anderson**
Ms. Anderson brings us several riveting tales of angelic intervention, from mysterious strangers helping lost hikers to outright divine intervention thwarting physical attack. The stories presented here are fascinating not only in their scope but also in the apparent sincerity of those who describe them. If you would like a good first-hand view of the angel phenomenon, this book is certainly a good place to begin your search.

***Touched by Angels: True Cases of Close Encounters of the Celestial Kind*. Aileen Elias Freeman**
Just to be clear, this book predates the popular CBS series *Touched by An Angel* by a few years and has no connection with that television show. Having that said, Ms. Freeman's book is full of great accounts of those who claim angels have directly intervened in their lives.

***In Search of Angels*. David Connolly**
Covering all aspects of the angel phenomenon from A to Z, this book serves as an excellent reference for all things angels. If you are interested in a little bit more background on angel lore, this book is a great place to start. It covers accounts of angels across

the three main monotheistic religions of Judaism, Christianity and Islam, with a few references to the ancient Persian (Iranian) religion of Zoroastrianism as well. This book is a great reference for anyone wanting to know the root source of belief in angels.

Angels: The Mysterious Messengers. Rex Hauck

Angels are much more than messengers, but their role as intercessors is certainly a major part of the angel story. This important aspect of angelic discourse is fully examined and explored in Mr. Hauck's book. From the first messengers of Holy Scripture to the continued ministry of angels as modern-day message bearers, it covers the entire history.

Angels in My Hair: The True Story of a Modern-Day Irish Mystic. Lorna Byrne

This book follows the story of Lorna Byrne, a middle-aged Irishwoman who sincerely believes that angels have been at her beck and call her entire life. Beginning in the crib, and all the way to her later years, she feels that she has been in communion with not just one guardian angel but an entire legion of them. Whether or not you believe everything she claims, the book is an absolutely fantastic read.

True Tales of Angel Encounters. Carmel Reilly

You will find a wide assortment of professed angel encounters in this angel anthology. Some are incredibly moving and powerful, and some are incredibly bizarre and flat-out odd. Either way, they're all great reads! This is one book that will definitely pique your interest in angels. Even the most ardent atheist and skeptic won't be able to put it down!

Where Angels Tread: Real Stories of Miracles and Angelic Intervention. Leslie Rule

This book goes case by case, following modern-day accounts of those who say they have been visited by angels. The stories are diverse, but they have many commonalities as well. If you would like to get an idea of just how angelic visitations allegedly happen, you should pick up this book.

***Heaven: Close Encounters of the God Kind.* Jesse Duplantis**
This book details the close encounters that televangelist Jesse Duplantis claims to have had with angels, God, and heaven. From watching Rev. Duplantis on TV, you would never imagine that he would claim such incredible things. He presents himself as more of a Christian stand-up comic than an experiencer of the profound. But while Rev. Duplantis isn't one to brag about his purported experiences, he lays it all out there in this book. Whether you believe it or not, the tales he tells are fascinating all the same.

www.mysteriousuniverse.com
This site has many useful accounts of alleged angelic visitations. If you are indeed curious about angels, this site will be of great interest to you. The stories are easy to find and catalogued by publication date. You can find many incredible firsthand accounts posted right here.

Also by Conrad Bauer

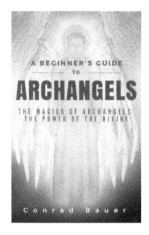

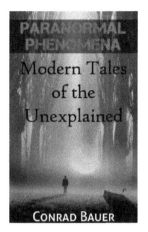

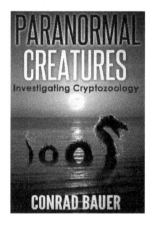

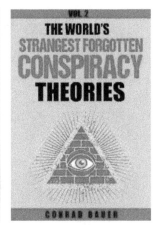

9 781721 665075